BROTHER | MATTHEW DICKMAN

Matthew Dickman is the author of *All-American Poem* (2008), *50 American Plays* (co-written with his twin brother Michael Dickman, 2012), *Mayakovsky's Revolver* (2012), *Wish You Were Here* (2013) and *24 HOURS* (2014). He is the recipient of the May Sarton Award from the American Academy of Arts and Sciences, the Kate Tufts Award from Claremont College and a 2015 Guggenheim award. Matthew Dickman is the Poetry Editor of *Tin House* magazine. He lives in Portland, Oregon.

'Matthew Dickman's all-American poems are the epitome of the pleasure principle; as clever as they are, they refuse to have ulterior intellectual pretensions; really, I think, they are spiritual in character – free and easy and unself-conscious, lusty, full of sensuous aspiration . . . We turn loose such poets into our culture so that they can provoke the rest of us into saying everything on our minds.'
  – Tony Hoagland, APR/Honickman First Book Prize judge

'[Matthew] Dickman crystallizes and celebrates human contact, reminding us . . . that our best memories, those most worth holding on to, those that might save us, will be memories of love . . . The background, then, is a downbeat America resolutely of the moment; the style, though, looks back to the singing free verse of Walt Whitman and Frank O'Hara . . . [Dickman's] work sings with all the crazy verve of the West.'
  – *Los Angeles Times*

T0333454

'Toughness with a smile . . . [Matthew Dickman] breathes the air of Whitman, Kerouac, O'Hara, and Koch, each of whom pushed against the grain of what poetry and writing was supposed to be in their times.'
  – *New Haven Review*

'One of America's most influential young poets . . . What fun there is in [Matthew] Dickman! What trouble and misery! There is enough sex and humor and beauty in these pages to make one swell with the ecstasy of existence. Yet, however natural the charm of Dickman's work, his poems are anything but naïve. His easy style may seem to look back at history with no more than an indifferent glance, but this insouciance is won through careful study: one of Dickman's magic tricks is pulling off the pose of footloose amateur while simultaneously engaging in a professional dialogue with the poetic tradition.'
  – *LA Review of Books*

'This is [Matthew] Dickman's skill. He tells you his story, intimately conversing with you as one would with an old friend, and he reminds you that although his poem seems to be about himself, what actually throbs beneath the language, words, and story, is an ache for his older brother. Dickman's conveyance of grief is not melodramatic or saccharine, he does not make sweeping proclamations. Instead, he is subtle.'
  – *The Rumpus*

MATTHEW DICKMAN

Brother

FABER & FABER

First published in 2016
by Faber & Faber Ltd
Bloomsbury House
74–77 Great Russell Street
London WC1B 3DA

Typeset by Faber & Faber Ltd
Printed in England by Martins the Printers, Berwick-upon-Tweed

'Cloud', 'Elegy to a Goldfish', 'Halcion', 'In Heaven', 'Notes Passed
to My Brother on the Occasion of His Funeral', 'On Earth' from
Mayakovsky's Revolver: Poems, copyright © 2012 by Matthew Dickman.
Used by permission of W. W. Norton & Company, Inc.

A CIP record for this book
is available from the British Library

ISBN 978–0–571–33020–1

2 4 6 8 10 9 7 5 3 1

for Dana Huddleston

Contents

BROTHER | MATTHEW DICKMAN

I hung pictures of you from every lamp post in town
— THE MOUNTAIN GOATS

Classical Poem

I'm listening to a symphony where heroes and villains are still alive.
Not a soundtrack of soldiers parachuting into occupied Belgium
but spies in pinstripes. Not a dark forest
lit up by gunfire and the wild eyes of a lost elk
but a dark alley, a cobblestone alley, an alley where important
documents are being passed between the black leather gloves
of important men
near a window where a barmaid is pouring beer into dirty glasses.
It's the kind of music to make love to
a tall skinny woman who works all day at the public library,
her breasts roaring like the two lions outside.
It's what I imagine astronauts are listening to
inside their helmets
while they watch a new planet begin to spin,
and then another and another like notes from a cello until the night sky
looks like an aquarium,
full of the mystical and unreal. Space dust
floating through a dark channel, a movable space
relaxing into itself. I'll tell you
the composer's name is Valentin Silvestrov
and I know as much about him as the umbrella I bought yesterday
knows about me. The radio program
says that this is the music of existential metaphor, silent songs,
which I do understand. I have them all the time.
When I first saw your feet, for instance. The curve and bright white
of them. The time you walked into my room

wearing your father's El Dorado hat and said
I am not my father. This is not his hat. Well, I thought,
you must be suffering
and it was life, the crestfallen drive-thru,
that was making you cry. But it was me.
And I'm no one in particular. I'm certainly not
Valentin Silvestrov living in '80s Berlin, all the West like a giant carrot
dangling in the blue sky and Rilke's angels
haunting him, following him
into the bathroom at night, waiting for him on the street
after someone the composer knew had died and it had, for this to be
    classical,
begun to snow. Heroes and villains killing each other in half
and quarter notes. Valentin putting on his greatcoat
with a rip in the lapel. Walking out toward the traffic. Walking home
and eventually laying down, like all of us, in the well-made, unbearable,
    bed.

Trouble

Marilyn Monroe took all her sleeping pills
to bed when she was thirty-six, and Marlon Brando's daughter
hung in the Tahitian bedroom
of her mother's house,
while Stanley Adams shot himself in the head. Sometimes
you can look at the clouds or the trees
and they look nothing like clouds or trees or the sky or the ground.
The performance artist Kathy Change
set herself on fire while Bing Crosby's sons shot themselves
out of the music industry forever.
I sometimes wonder about the inner lives of polar bears. The French
philosopher Gilles Deleuze jumped
from an apartment window into the world
and then out of it. Peg Entwistle, an actress with no lead
roles, leaped off the H in the HOLLYWOOD sign
when everything looked black and white
and David O. Selznick was king, circa 1932. Ernest Hemingway
put a shotgun to his head in Ketchum, Idaho
while his granddaughter, a model and actress, climbed the family tree
and overdosed on phenobarbital. My brother opened
thirteen fentanyl patches and stuck them on his body
until it wasn't his body anymore. I like
the way geese sound above the river. I like
the little soaps you find in hotel bathrooms because they're beautiful.
Sarah Kane hanged herself, Harold Pinter
brought her roses when she was still alive,

and Louis Lingg, the German anarchist, lit a cap of dynamite
in his own mouth
though it took six hours for him
to die, 1887. Ludwig II of Bavaria drowned
and so did Hart Crane, John Berryman, and Virginia Woolf. If you are
traveling, you should always bring a book to read, especially
on a train. Andrew Martinez, the nude activist, died
in prison, naked, a bag
around his head, while in 1815 the Polish aristocrat and writer
Jan Potocki shot himself with a silver bullet.
Sara Teasdale swallowed a bottle of blues
after drawing a hot bath,
in which dozens of Roman senators opened their veins beneath the water.
Larry Walters became famous
for flying in a Sears patio chair and forty-five helium-filled
weather balloons. He reached an altitude of 16,000 feet
and then he landed. He was a man who flew.
He shot himself in the heart. In the morning I get out of bed, I brush
my teeth, I wash my face, I get dressed in the clothes I like best.
I want to be good to myself.

Grief

When grief comes to you as a purple gorilla
you must count yourself lucky.
You must offer her what's left
of your dinner, the book you were trying to finish
you must put aside,
and make her a place to sit at the foot of your bed,
her eyes moving from the clock
to the television and back again.
I am not afraid. She has been here before
and now I can recognize her gait
as she approaches the house.
Some nights, when I know she's coming,
I unlock the door, lie down on my back,
and count her steps
from the street to the porch.
Tonight she brings a pencil and a ream of paper,
tells me to write down
everyone I have ever known,
and we separate them between the living and the dead
so she can pick each name at random.
I play her favorite Willie Nelson album
because she misses Texas
but I don't ask why.
She hums a little,
the way my brother does when he gardens.
We sit for an hour

while she tells me how unreasonable I've been,
crying in the checkout line,
refusing to eat, refusing to shower,
all the smoking and all the drinking.
Eventually she puts one of her heavy
purple arms around me, leans
her head against mine,
and all of a sudden things are feeling romantic.
So I tell her,
things are feeling romantic.
She pulls another name, this time
from the dead,
and turns to me in that way that parents do
so you feel embarrassed or ashamed of something.
Romantic? she says,
reading the name out loud, slowly,
so I am aware of each syllable, each vowel
wrapping around the bones like new muscle,
the sound of that person's body
and how reckless it is,
how careless that his name is in one pile and not the other.

We Are Not Temples

My friend, a Buddhist, tells me
that life is constantly changing
and that my struggle against it
is the cause of all my suffering. That and wanting
what I do not have, being less than excited about what I do,
and the shaky delusions
of an invented reality in which I probably live
most of my days. She's right.
Life changes. The sacred becomes, after many years, secular
and then turns back around as if it has forgotten its keys,
becoming sacred all over again.
It's like Florida when it was wild and native,
with turkey-skinned, sun-burned Europeans.
Tropical diseases running willy-nilly through everyone's veins
until, once upon a time, Mr Walt Disney
or Mr Walt Disney's children built their castles
and tea-cup rides, making a trip to Florida almost as sacramental
as it was commercial. I'm the same way,
depending on who's loving me
or hating me, taking my letters and burning them,
ripping them up, throwing them in the air
above a bed we might have shared
while a friend cheers on, yelling *that's right – you go girl!*
And it is right, necessary even, fuck – if I was there
listening to the Indigo Girls and drinking Chardonnay
I'd rip my letters up too. As for the invented reality

I live in, my friend is also correct. I am so much bigger
than in real life. I've played lead guitar
for famous bands, I've played lead roles
in famous movies, I've been in outer space and I've been a pig
farmer with a beautiful wife from Ireland.
But those, perhaps, are not delusions as much as they are dreams.
Not so much Florida without Disney World,
its five-dollar soft drinks and coked-out Donald Ducks
posing with five hundred sticky kids
but Florida with Seminole Indians and Sun Dances.
As far as delusions go
it must be the ones I have about kindness,
that I am never mean or have never wanted to disgrace
your wife in the coat room of a community theater.
Or that I would always give up my seat
on the bus for the elderly woman who grumbles
about how much she hates Mexicans,
that I move so that others can be more free,
that my body is a temple,
a kind of Taj Mahal or Mall of America,
where people come to pray
and spend money, where I put the wholesome
offerings of high-fructose corn syrup
and carcinogens onto the altars of the lung and liver,
that I never wanted what my cousins have, their completeness
and money. Their beauty. Things like that.
Small things. Big things.
This must be why my Buddhist friend is concerned,
as she smokes her American Spirit
cigarettes. Which is not to say she's a hypocrite

or delusional
or is in any way linked to the suffering
of Native Americans,
though it might be some peculiar destiny
that one people would be dying of alcoholism
while the other succumbs to lung cancer, what it is,
as the blue smoke exhales from her small chest
which is covered, this evening, in a creamy silk top
with spaghetti straps, what it is is that we are not temples,
our bodies, no matter how many worms
work all night to make a sexy, creamy silk top
with spaghetti straps, a kind of industrial workmanship
outdone, by the way,
only through the greater exertion
of the twelve-year-old Taiwanese
who put the damn things together. No, our bodies are chemical,
organic bed and breakfasts, where we stay out too late on the beaches
of our desires and in the morning over a plate of scrambled eggs
and a hot cup of caffeine-enriched coffee,
we come running into the Shangri-La that is sober advice.
Or we meet in a bar like this one with our sacred prayer beads
in one hand and the now secular tobacco
in the other, inhaling it,
and then letting it exhale slowly like the long breath
those first men and women from Cheap End must have taken
when they walked off the plank of their Dickensian ships
and onto the sands of the untouched, divine, and humid Floridian coast.

In Heaven

No dog chained to a spike in a yard of dying
grass like the dogs
I grew up with, starving, overfed, punched in the face
by children, no children, no firecrackers
slipped down the long throats of bottles in the first days of summer,
no sky exploding, no blood, no bones
because we were the bones, no more Lord
my God, or maps made of fire, a small blaze burning
right where I grew up, so I could,
if I wanted to, point to the flame that was 82nd Avenue,
no milk in the fridge, no more walking through the street
to the little store
that sold butterfly knives, no more knives, no more honey
now that all the sweetness is gone, though we were the sweetness,
though we needed something
for our tongues, no more cheap soap, no more
washing our mouths out
because Motherfucker and because Fuck Off
came swimming out of us like fish from the Pacific Ocean,
no hummingbirds, no Band-Aids, no scraped knees
with the dirt and rock from the neighborhood
because we were the dirt,
no young mothers smoking cigarettes on the porch
while the sky got pretty
before night came on, though they were prettier
and the sky turned against them. No punk rock, no prom,

no cheap high heels left in the rain
in a parking lot, no empty bottles of wine coolers
because we were the empty bottles, no throwing them against the wall
behind the school because we were the glass
that was shattering. No more looking toward the west, no east, no north
or south, just us standing here together, asking each other
if we remember anything, what we loved, what loved us, who yelled our
    names first?

Halcion

You are the illuminated world, floating ballroom, spark and flash,
cold December star above the hospital,
moonlit pond, little boat, your waters calm
as a spoon. I've never been higher.
I can feel you melt on my tongue like a naked girl wearing a diamond
crown, standing barefoot on a bed
of ice, her eyes turning white, her body a cloud broken by lightning,
glowing like a nurse in a dark hall. You turn
all my emergencies into cotton, all my fainting into land, my blue boy
at the bottom of a paper cup, you make the meadow
bright, make me brave. Now I can walk
through the land of strangers and freeways, surgery and rubber gloves,
the panic, the knife, the ambulance of dawn,
the gurney being lifted into the air. When I'm made to lie down
on the metal bed, when the first tube is threaded through me, I want you
my cherry blossom season, my dream of gauze and light, your petals
   swirling
around my feet, IVs and Jell-O, Tu Fu singing at the edge of the Yangtze
   forever.

Notes Passed to My Brother on the Occasion of His Funeral

1 My Brother's Grave

Like a city I've always hated, driving through but never stopping,
my foot on the gas, running all the lights,
wishing I were home. Hating even the children who live there
as if they had a choice. I imagine him
in his ten-million particles
of ash, tied up into a beautiful white bundle of lace, a silver bow
looped where his neck should be,
thrown into a washing machine, set on a delicate cycle
to spin forever under the dirt. The all of him
left, the vegetation of him, the no more thing
of him: his skateboard and mountain bike and beers and cigarettes
    and daughter
and mix-tapes and loneliness, his legs and feet and arms and brain
    and kneecaps.
Outside the graveyard
there is still some part of him
buried in the mysticism of his DNA, smeared across a doorknob
or brushed along the jagged edge of his car keys. Two kids
from the high school nearby
will fuck each other on top of him
and I won't know how to stop them. Someone
will throw an empty bottle of vodka over their shoulder
and he will have to catch it.

2 Coffee

The only precious thing I own, this little espresso
cup. And in it a dark roast all the way
from Honduras, Guatemala, Ethiopia
where coffee was born in the ninth century
getting goat herders high, spinning like dervishes,
the white blooms cresting out
of the evergreen plant, Ethiopia
where I almost lived for a moment but
then the rebels surrounded the Capital
so I stayed home and drank
coffee and listened to the radio
and heard how they were getting along. I would walk
down Everett Street, near the hospital
where my brother was bound
to his white bed like a human mast, where he was
getting his mind right and learning
not to hurt himself. I would walk by and be afraid and smell
the beans being roasted inside the garage
of an old warehouse. It smelled like burnt
toast! It was everywhere in the trees. I couldn't
bear to see him. Sometimes
he would call. He wanted us
to sit across from each other, coffee between us,
sober. Coffee can taste like grapefruit
or caramel, like tobacco, strawberry,
cinnamon, the oils being pushed
out of the grounds and floating to the top of a French press,

the expensive kind I get in the mail,
the mailman waking me up
from a night when all I had was tea
and watched a movie about the Queen of England
when Spain was hot
for all her castles and all their ships, carved out
of fine Spanish trees, went up in flames
while back home Spaniards were growing potatoes
and coffee was making its careful way
along a giant whip
from Africa to Europe
where cafes would become famous
and people would eventually sit
with their cappuccinos, the barista
talking about the new war, a cup of sugar
on the table, a curled piece of lemon rind. A beret
on someone's head, a scarf
around their neck, a bomb in a suitcase
left beneath a small table. Right now
I'm sitting near a hospital where psychotropics are being
carried down the hall in a pink cup,
where someone is lying there and he doesn't know who
he is. I'm listening
to the couple next to me
talk about their cars. I have no idea
how I got here. The world stops at the window
while I take my little spoon and slowly swirl the cream around the lip
of the cup. Once, I had a brother
who used to sit and drink his coffee black, smoke
his cigarettes and be quiet for a moment

before his brain turned its armadas against him, wanting to burn down
his cities and villages, before grief
became his capital with its one loyal flag and his face,
perhaps only his beautiful left eye,
shimmering on the surface of his Americano
like a dark star.

3 Mayakovsky's Revolver

I keep thinking about the way
blackberries will make the mouth
of an eight-year-old look like he's a ghost
that's been shot in the face. In the dark I can see
my older brother walking through the tall brush
of his brain. I can see him standing
in the lobby of the hotel,
alone, crying along with the ice machine.
Instead of the moon
I've been falling for the lunar light pouring out of a plastic shell
I've plugged into the bathroom wall. Online
someone is claiming to own Mayakovsky's revolver
which they will sell for only fifty thousand dollars. Why didn't I
think of that? Remove the socks from my dead brother's feet
and trade them in for a small bit
of change, a ticket to a movie, something
with a receipt, proof I was busy living,
that I didn't stay in all night weeping,
that I didn't stay up
drawing a gun over and over
with a black marker, that I didn't cut
out the best one, or stand
in front of the mirror, pulling the paper trigger until it tore away.

4 More Than One Life

My older brother is standing outside the movie theater like a man
I have never met. Standing in the snow, looking up
at posters for films
that haven't played in over fifty years. In this dream
he's thirteen years old
and then he's thirty, and then he's nothing. John Wayne
is looking down at him and so is Greta Garbo. Here in New York
Marlene Dietrich is inhaling all the death
a close-up can gather in its big, beautiful, hazy arms. My brother
has lit a cigarette.
He's turning up his collar.
He looks like Gary Cooper. He flicks the butt into the street
like a detective, his long fingers making a shadow
across the sidewalk. In this life
nothing inside him wants to pull a knife, load a gun, open a package
of pain killers. In this life he has a day off
and is going to see a movie and buy some popcorn and sit in a darkness
he can rise from, and walk up the aisle like a groom, walk
out into the air again, and down the street, and whistle maybe, and
   go home.

5 I Feel Like the Galaxy

You have not died yet. Instead,
you are walking down Thirteenth Avenue
drinking your coffee,
thinking about death, all the different ways,
all the opportunities glimmering
ahead of you, thinking about the woman
who poured your coffee. The woman
at the cafe who asked if you needed
a receipt, rang you up
and took your credit card,
is a love you will never have
though somewhere in your brain
her long hair is living out
a dream of wheat, her dress,
how it must feel
around her, snug and slippery, is falling
behind you, almost forgotten,
so now you can get back to it, death,
your little love, your hot nipple-action
of fear, a train
in the dark before it breaks, rising up as you
cross the food carts on Alder
and head for the park. There's a garbage can
near the west entrance where you throw away
your empty cup. Maybe,
because you are wearing your new shoes,
you are not heading east

toward a ceiling fan and pills,
toward a six-pack and medicated patches.
I lost you to a bar
and an all-night record store. Lost you
to an old Beastie Boys T-shirt and shredding
punk rock guitar. I found you in a tin can
of cigarette butts
beside the door to the AA meeting
where our sister is standing up and walking
to the back of the room
for more coffee. I found you in my kitchen,
in the handle of a knife, I found you
sitting on my bed, right in the middle, a shadow
made of air and dust. The galaxy's
lifting me across the street. You
should come back from this deep-sea dive, rise
up in your turn-of-the-century scuba gear
while I stand on the prow
of the ship, making sure the oxygen is flowing
down the black rubber tube into the black
of where you are. You should come back
from the fields with your pockets
full of grain, your feet covered in hardened clay, back
from the planet
you discovered but never had time
to name, you should land
in my backyard at night, an earth landing, a triumph
of science and engineering, the rockets
cooling as the door of your spaceship
makes a great sucking sound

and begins to lower, the lights
from inside the vessel
lighting up the back porch and fence and you
walking out in your silver uniform
or in the green and gray body, the silky wet skin
of an alien. I will take you back
any way you want, I will look into your diamond-
shaped face, into your glowing
egg-large eyes and still recognize you, still
open a beer and sit close
in the yard while you pick at the grass,
staring up at the sky, and cry and scream for missing it.

6 Satellite

I'm sitting beneath the bent
live oak, wishing the plane blinking above me
was a satellite that would shoot images
of my older brother back down into my brain
so I could print them out
and paste them on the wall. I have to
keep looking at this one picture of him
to remember how his jaw was and which side of the moon
he parted his hair. He's always
away from me now, some animal or constellation
that walked out of the world but for rumors
and half skeletons found in the Congo, drawings
of what they might have looked like. My brain dreams
about cities from outer space, a place with a name
like Kilimanjaro where he might still be walking around in his Vision
Street Wear high tops, or even a shadow like my father
who talked about Costco the night of my brother's cremation and how
pumpkiny the pumpkin pie was
though he bought it in a frozen pack of twenty. Just like a real bakery,
he said, you just throw it in the oven,
he kept saying that, you just throw it in the oven, you just throw it in
    the oven.

7 West Hills

My older brother is in heaven
above the West Hills, swimming
in a swimming pool, behind a big house
built on the side of a hill
on stilts so it won't go crashing down
into the long boulevard below it. Built that way
so the house won't jump, won't one day decide
it's over, nothing left, the dark from the evergreen trees
making it all seem like closets and midnight.
My brother on his back looking up at the sky. He's full
of cocaine and Heineken. There is no telling him apart
from the sun or the sky or the shining stars his hands make,
the water falling from his fingers
back into the wet body of the pool. Whenever I drive up here,
through the black curves, I wonder which house it is,
which one became a kind of vacation
for his heart, what the bathroom looks like, whose bottle
of Vicodin he carried between the soft skin of his waist and the elastic
band of his swim trunks, if that person was a woman, if she was beautiful,
if later she pulled him, soaking, past the leather furniture,
past the mirrors and Chinese vases throwing up their long silvery petals,
into the bedroom and then knelt down
in front of his body which by then was all electricity and chemical halos, if
she took his shorts by the waist or by the pockets, if she knew he was already
stuffing his wrists with razors
like strange envelopes or building the pyramids
of pills that would take him to Tutankhamen, that he was planning his
New Kingdom, if she listened to his breathing all night or if she knew his name.

8 Pants

Walking through the snow
all the cars look like flying saucers. Planets are becoming
stars again. The lovers on Mars are spooning
in their beds, their soft green
heads on something like a pillow of Northern Lights. Things
feel dangerous without you and far away.
Space dust floating above
the Event Horizon, bodies falling from the windows
on earth. Last night
I stopped smoking so now everything will get really-really sad
until my body is done
punishing itself for punishing itself. I have a pair of pants
I work in and a pair I've never worn. I have a pair
I bought in Austin
when the only thing on my mind was Susan. Susan!
She wore these lovely cotton slacks like Katharine Hepburn
but was Jewish
which made her even more beautiful –
some fascist inside me
watching the History Channel and romanticizing tragedy.
Like when they took my brother's body
away and I stood in the house folding a pair of his pants.
I felt so alien and special
placing one leg over the other
and then folding them at the knee like a priest
removing his vestments and kissing the long silk scarf
before gently placing it on an altar
built for a man no one ever knew, not even his father, who wasn't there.

9 The Bomb

On December twenty-second I walked out
into the street and said your name three times,
slowly, with my eyes closed, then looked down where the road
stops at the pasture and waited for you
to climb over the barbed-wire fence in your bare feet, in the jeans
you wore when you stopped breathing. For a month now
when people say your name I think of a ladder coming up
out of the sea with a small boy
appearing, one foot at a time, looking toward
the coast and then back toward the horizon
and then climbing beneath the surf,
his soft hair floating on the surface before he disappears entirely.
I've been watching a Spanish movie
about ghosts. In it a bomb has landed in the courtyard
of a boys' school
but has never gone off, half in the ground and half in the air. Sometimes
the bravest boys will come up to it
and slap it with their hands. The bomb echoes
and the world gets tested. Men
ride out of a green forest on brown horses
and the bomb just sits there
like an old bell, like a body someone has found
and wondering if it's alive
picks up a stick and pokes it in the leg, the stomach,
the shoulder, the face, and if he's mean or just alone he might try to open
one of the eyes, or kick the body to see how it feels, to see if a sound
    comes out.

10 King

I'm always the king of something. Ruined or celebrated,
newly crowned, or just beheaded. King of the shady grass
and king of the dirty sheets. I sit in the middle
of the room in December
with the windows open, five pills and a razor. My lifelong
secret. My killing power and my staying
power. When the erection fails, when the car almost hits
the divider, I'm king. I wave my hand over
the ants bubbling out of the sidewalk and make them all knights,
I sit at the dinner table and look into the deep
dark eyes of my television, my people. I tell them the kingdom
will be remembered in dreams of static. I tell them
what was lost will be found. So I put on my black-white
checkered vans, the exact pair of shoes
my older brother wore when he was still a citizen in the world
and I go out, I go out into the street
with my map of the dead and look for him,
for the X he is,
so I can put the scepter back in his hands, take the red
cloak from my shoulders and put it around his, lift the crown
from my head and fit it just above his eyebrows,
so I can get down on one knee, on both
knees, and lower my face and whisper my lord, my master, my king.

11 *Field*

I'm standing in the field
trying to figure out if there was a difference
for my older brother, the first time he cut himself,
between his body as a battlefield
and his body as a battleground. The moon
is wearing a white kimono that covers most of her
legs. I always knew she was Japanese! I will have to stand here
a long time if I want to learn something, if I want to
transform myself into some kind of superhero for the living,
someone that wears a cape
and fights crime, cures cancer, makes
you feel like you've been bathing in blowjobs and mescaline.
I want, I want, I need! I want the ground
my brother is buried in
to be the field that I am standing on. So we can be together.
So I can bend down
and put my face into the grass. So that
when the wind picks up like Halloween
he'll hear me saying to him *did you feel that? Wasn't that spooky?*

12 Dog

I'm hiding from the stars tonight. I've pulled
every blind and turned off
all the lights but one, which I've named after you,
which I can see flooding the dark
hallway of my high school when I open the locker
with your name on it, the only one
left, the universe flooding out
onto the floor. In all the pictures
I've seen of my older brother
he is never wearing a tuxedo. But I have one snapshot, bent
at the edges, of my twin and me
on a boat, on prom night, happy, already a little drunk.
I carry this picture whenever I fly
so I can look at it right before the crash, below the screams
and the smell of urine, I can look into his eyes
and know who I am. All night I've been worrying
about money and cancer and the tooth
I have to get pulled out before it poisons me. I can smell
the lemon I cut earlier for the carrots and fish. I don't know
what to do with myself. I've written the word Choose
on a piece of paper and taped it to a knife. Then I peeled it off
and taped it to a book about Yesenin. Finally
I took it and stuck it on the screen
of my computer where there is a picture of Erika wearing the silver
necklace I bought her. Outside a dog is sitting in the yard
looking up at the porch. Every once in a while
it wags its tail and whines, then it's quiet, and then it begins to growl.

13 Anything You Want

My living brother
is treating us to dinner. He opens the menu wide like a set of wings
across the table. Anything you want
he says. His voice warm
above the shining heaven of the silverware. The other one,
my dead brother, is sitting
in the dark in the graveyard, his back leaning back against his name.
I'm walking by with my favorite drug
inside me. He's picking at a scab on his wrist.
He looks up, opens his arms
wide above the grass. Anything you want, he says. His body beginning
to wash out, his voice slowly crawling back.

Cloud

I found a white piece of paper
with your name on it,
your old phone number written in the dark
loop of your handwriting.
I was standing outside a restaurant
watching this one cloud
float by like foam on a pint of beer
and thinking about how good
you've become at not being here anymore, how you
finally broke
like a storm across the sky of everything. The clouds are not moving
in slow motion. In fact the clouds are very fast
and have somewhere to go,
some tornado or other to take care of, to urge on.
This cloud is a rain cloud with a razor
in its pocket. It has followed me around all day
and all day clouds rose above my head and disappeared,
as I lit and relit a cigarette. The smoke
looked like the blue eyes of a fish. A metal
blue ruining the sky, I remember
lying down on the roof of the Portlandia Building,
my high school girlfriend
throwing pennies off the side because she heard somewhere
it could kill a person
if it fell far enough and asking me if I could be anyone, who would I be?
I thought of you, lost in a sheet

somewhere, the nurse in her white arch supports,
the trees outside your window making hay
with the sky, your body clouding up, your medication floating off
into a field somewhere full of cows
with eyes and brains and the slow life
I imagine god enjoys
because when it comes to god his hospital is a field, his imagination
    a bovine.

Elegy to a Goldfish

I can't remember when
my brother and I decided to kill you, small
fish with no school, bright and happy at the bottom,
slipping through the gate
of your fake castle. I think it was winter. A part of us
aware of the death outside, the leaves
being burned up and the squirrels starving
inside the oaks, the sky
knocking its clouds into the ashtray of the city.
And it might have been me
who picked you up first, who
chased you around the clean bowl of your life
and brought you up into the suffocating
elevator of ours. And I want to say it was my brother
who threw you against the wall
like a drunk husband, the glow-worm inch of you
sliding down the English Garden
of wallpaper, and that it was me who raised my leg
like a dog, me who brought my bare foot
slamming down on your almost nothing ribs,
and felt you smear like a pimple. Now that's something
I get to have forever. That Halloween-candy-
sized rage, that cough drop
of meanness. And your death, only
the beginning, the mushy orange autopsy
reminded us of Mandarins, Navels, Bloods, Persians,

the sweet Valencia. And when our sister,
who must have thought of you all day,
came home to find the bowl
empty, looked at us, my brother and me,
I remember we started to laugh. And then
it might have been me,
though it could have been him, who thought to open
the can of tangerines, who pulled
one of the orange bodies out of the syrup, and threw it at her,
this new artificial you, chasing her around the house
screaming Eat him! Eat him!
but it was me who held her down on her bed
and him who forced
her mouth open, and it was me who pushed
the sticky fruit into her throat
like a bloody foot
into a sock. You had only been gone for one hour
and yet the sky outside
turned black and red, the tree in the yard thrashed back
and forth until its spinal cord
broke, and my little sister, your one love, flashed white
and pulsed like neon
in a hospital, her eyes
rolling back into the aquarium of her head
for a moment, and in every country
countless deaths, but none as important
as yours, tiny Christ, machine of hope, martyr of girls and boys.

On Earth

My little sister walks away
from the crash, the black ice, the crushed passenger
side, the eighteen-wheeler that destroyed
the car, and from a ditch on the side of the highway
a white plastic bag floating up
out of the grass
where the worms are working slow and blind beneath
the ants that march
in their single columns of grace like soldiers
before they're shipped out, before war makes them human
again and scatters them across the fields
and the sands, across stretchers and bodies,
across the universe
of smoke and ash, makes them crouch down
in what's left of a building
while a tank moves up the street toward the river
where it will stop, turn its engine off, the driver looking
through a window smaller than an envelope,
where he will sweat and think
about how beautiful Kentucky is. On earth
my twin brother gets his cancer cut out
of his forehead after a year of picking at it and me
always saying 'hey! Don't pick at your cancer!'
but joking because he can never be sick,
not if I want to stay on earth,
and my little sister can never be torn in half, a piece of her

used Subaru separating her torso
from her legs, not if I want to live, not if I want to walk
across the Hawthorne Bridge
with the city ahead of me, the buildings
full of light and elevators, the park full of maples
and benches, the police filling up
the streets like Novocain, numbing
Chinatown, numbing Old Town, the Willamette
running toward the wild
Pacific, the great hydro-adventure North
still pulling at the blood of New Yorkers and New Englanders,
the logging gone and the Indians gone
but for casinos and fireworks and dream-catchers,
my little sister has to rise from the dead
steel and broken headlights, my twin brother
has to get himself down from the operating table
if I'm going to be able to watch the rainclouds come in
like a family of hippos
from the warm waters of Africa
and dry off in the dust, they have to be here
if I'm going to write a letter
to Marie or Dorianne, Michael and Elizabeth
have to be in their bodies
for me not to cut them
out of my own. They have to answer
the phone when I call for me not to walk into the closet
forever. Right now I am sitting
on the porch of the house I grew up in. The second place
I was on earth! The porch where Emily sat
in 1994, drinking licorice tea

and reading Rexroth's translations of Li Po,
some Chinese poetry
in the curve of her foot, the Han River
spilling out of her hair, over the steps,
and into the driveway
where the Dandelions grew like white blood
cells. I would pick them in Kelly Park
and I would walk along the street with them
on 92nd. All my wishes, all of them floating out
over a neighborhood
where I wanted to be in love
with someone, drinking orange sodas on our backs
with the sky unbuttoning our jeans
and pulling off our shirts. There's nothing
like walking through Northwest Portland
at night, even though it's sick with money
and doesn't look like itself. There's nothing on earth
like the moonlight, lake at night
smell of tall grass and suntan lotion. It's hard to imagine
not knowing the smell of gas stations or pine,
the smell of socks worn too long and the smell
of someone's hands
after they have swam through a rosemary bush.
I want them all
and all the time. I need to walk
into Erika's room, over the piles of clothes on the floor
which I love for their pyramid euphoria. I need to
smell her body on mine
days after we have destroyed the bed or ruined the carpet
she hates unless we are on it. On earth

my older sister can never open another bottle of beer, shoot
another glass of whiskey. She can't have the monster
of her body go slouching through
the countryside of her family, killing the peasants,
burning the fields along the road to another sobriety
and then be hacked to death by her own pitchforks and spades,
not if I want to brush my teeth
without biting off my tongue. Not if I want to drink coffee
and read the paper and breathe. Oh to be on earth.
To walk barefoot on the cold stone
and know that the woman you love is also walking barefoot
on the cold tile in the kitchen
where you kissed her yesterday, to be standing in a bookstore
and smell the old paper and the glue
in the spines, to look at a map of a strange city
and be able to figure out
where it is you're going. To swim in the ocean,
to swim in a lake and not know
what's beneath you. To have two thousand
friends on Facebook you don't know
but stare at every night because you're lonely.
To walk through
Laurelhurst and see a blue heron
killing a bright orange fish, lifting it into the suffocating air
and then drowning it again, and then the air,
and back and forth until it feels
the fish is hers completely. To feel how the subway is racing
beneath an avenue
or how the plane that took off from New York is doing
well in the sky over Arizona. To know

how it feels after drinking whiskey or that secretly reading
Romance novels has made you
into a kinder, gentler, person, walking through
the grocery store in the middle of the night,
in love with avocados and carrots,
standing in front of the frozen fruit
with the glass door open
so the cold frozen food air can cool your body down
before you walk through the cereal aisle
with it's innumerable colors and kinds, how a box of cereal
feels in your hands
like an award you've received for some great service, to wait
in line at the checkout and not care that you
have to wait. The feeling of being on a boat
and the feeling of putting on new shoes
with a metal shoehorn. How you feel like you can run
faster than you ever have. To get on a bus in winter
and have your glasses steam up, the bus
taking you down the street you have known all your life
or only just found but love all the same. On earth
my mother is talking to her breasts
because they want to kill her, they have turned against her
like a Senate, but in the end
she talks them out of it. She makes them behave like two dogs
or like children playing
too rough with the cat and the cat screaming, her tail almost
pulled off. She has to still be here, taking
the Lloyd Center exit to work
in the rain, if I'm going to live at all. On earth
I have a bed I can't wait to get into, the clean smell of white

sheets, letting my head fall
onto the soft pillow and worry and pull
the blanket over, like a grave,
and in the morning watch the cold winter light
blowing in through the window. Every night the dark
and every morning the light
and you don't think Jesus walked out
of his cave, crawled out of his Subaru
and stood on the side of the road for the ambulance to come
and cover him in a white shroud? On earth
I faint in the lobby of the multiplex, pee my pants, go into a seizure
like someone talking in tongues, wrapped
in the flames of belief, my body held in the hands of strangers
above the old shag carpet
while on earth the popcorn is popping wildly
and the licorice is bright red
beneath the glass counter, next to the M&Ms
where the most beautiful girl in the world is standing
in her stiff uniform, her nametag
pinned tight, her name written on a piece of tape
that covers someone else's name.
She will never kiss me, never lie in bed with August outside
and whisper my name. On earth
Joe has a heart attack, his pack of unfiltered cigarettes
resting like a hand near his books.
He rides his heart through the three acres of bypass
and then leads it to water. On earth
I steal flowers from the park, roses and star lilies,
I sleep too much. I'm always too slow
or arriving too early, before anything has opened. I keep

dreaming my older brother
has come back like a man returned from a long, exhausting,
run. I can't do this much longer!
And because I don't have to, I cut an orange
the way athletes do, into perfect
half moons. I peel the pulp away, the skin that looks like
the surface of the moon. I put each one
inside my mouth
and let the sex of it burst into my throat, my lungs
like two black halves of a butterfly
trapped in the net of my chest, I read a poem
Zach wrote about a pond, I'm thinking
about the last time I saw Mike
before he moved into the Zion-air of Utah, I reread
a note Carl wrote that only says
beware. On earth Charlie is cut open
and put back together.
He goes on loving his friends and looking into the mirror,
and maybe the nerves have not grown back
over the river the scar has made, and maybe he is tired
but on earth! He has to get up in the morning
if I'm going to lie on my bed
listening to records with the window open
and the door open and wait
in my boxers for love to enter in her dirty feet
and sweaty hands, if I'm going to pull her near me, my mouth
over a knuckle, my hand beneath her knee, he has to
still be here. On earth
survival is built out of luck and treatment centers
or slow like a planet being born, before

there was anyone to survive,
the gases of the Big Bang just settling, or it's built
like a skyscraper, by hand, some workmen
falling, and some safe on the scaffold, up above the earth,
unwrapping the sandwiches they have been waiting all day to eat.

'[Michael] Dickman (like a host of other white-spacers before and with him) invites me to participate in the construction of memory, of perception, in something that feels like real time . . . It's been some time since I encountered a poetry that, rather than talk to me or think at me, asked me to try on its body. I like it.'
  – *Poetry*

'Reading Michael is like stepping out of an overheated apartment building to be met, unexpectedly, by an exhilaratingly chill gust of wind.'
  – *The New Yorker*

BROTHER | MICHAEL DICKMAN

Michael Dickman is the author of three books of poems, *The End of the West* (2009), *Flies* (2011, Winner of the James Laughlin Award), and *Green Migraine* (2015), as well as a book of plays, *50 American Plays*, co-written with his twin brother, Matthew Dickman, in 2012. He lives in Princeton, New Jersey, where he is on the faculty at Princeton University.

'Elizabeth Bishop said that the three qualities she admired most in poetry were accuracy, spontaneity, and mystery. Michael Dickman's first full-length collection of poems demonstrates each brilliantly . . . These are lithe, seemingly effortless poems, poems whose strange affective power remains even after several readings . . . one of the most accomplished and original poets to emerge in years.'
  – *Believer*

'Hilarity transfiguring all that dread, manic overflow of powerful feeling, zero at the bone – *Flies* renders its desolation with singular invention and focus and figuration: the making of these poems makes them exhilarating.'
  – James Laughlin Award citation

'A hushed book that is nevertheless full of lines like fish breaking the surface of a still pond . . . This is only Dickman's second book, but like his twin, Matthew, he already seems a major American talent.'
  – *New York Times*

MICHAEL DICKMAN

Brother

ff

FABER & FABER

First published in 2016
by Faber & Faber Ltd
Bloomsbury House
74–77 Great Russell Street
London WC1B 3DA

Typeset by Faber & Faber Ltd
Printed in England by Martins the Printers, Berwick-upon-Tweed

'Nervous System', 'Kings' and 'We Did Not Make Ourselves' from *The End
of the West*, copyright © 2009 by Michael Dickman. 'Dead Brother Super Hero',
'False Start', 'Flies', 'Ralph Eugene Meatyard: Untitled', 'The New Green',
'Killing Flies' and 'Home' from *Flies*, copyright © 2011 by Michael Dickman.
All reprinted with the permission of The Permissions Company, Inc., on behalf
of Copper Canyon Press, www.coppercanyonpress.org.

A CIP record for this book
is available from the British Library

ISBN 978-0-571-33020-1

2 4 6 8 10 9 7 5 3 1

for Dana Huddleston

Contents

BROTHER | MICHAEL DICKMAN

you should write to your brother
every night
        until he recovers
  — PERFUME GENIUS

Nervous System

Make a list
of everything that's
ever been

on fire –

Abandoned cars
Trees
The sea

Your mother burned down to a skeleton

So she could come back born back from her bed and walk around the
    house again
    exhausted in slippers

What else?

Your brain
Your eyes
Your lungs

*

When you look down
inside yourself
what is there?

You are a walking bag of surgical instruments
shining from the inside out
and that's just today

Tomorrow it could be different

When I think of the childhood inside me I think of sunlight dying on
   a windowsill

The voices of my friends
in the sunlight

All of us
running around
outside our deaths

*

Someone is here
to see you
again

Someone has come a long way with their arms out in front of them like
  a child

walking down a hallway
at night

Make room for them –
they're very tired

I wish I could look down past the burning chandelier inside me

where the language begins
to end and

down

Kings

Our crowns look nothing like his crown

Needles and light and
needles *of* light
fingers
stamen

Our crowns are made of dead hair and get swept out with the trash or
ripped out by hand

Bath-towels or capes
wrapped around our necks
and fastened with
giant safety pins

Not ermine not
rabbits

I ran around the neighborhood playing King of the Block
in my red underwear

The trees didn't bow
I was not on fire as he
passed by

*

None of my friends are kings anymore

They used to be good at being alive pointing their index fingers at the
    trees passing invisible sentences

proclamations
knighting the birds
one by one

All down my street the new fathers
beat the kingness
out
of the
kings

when they came in for dinner
and when they
went to bed

The birds knocking against the windows in the wind

and he wasn't in the wind

*

When I think of him now all alone
he looks like a mouse

King of the Mice

He's white like we all thought
red eyes
red tongue
yellow teeth

Scampering across the kitchen floor in the middle of the night when we
    wake up and want to make a sandwich

Listen
when you turn back into nothing and disappear forever
down a hole in the floor
I want to go with you

But we can't go

What a motherfucker that is

The kitchen window
the only light
for blocks

Now we're going to know what it feels like

We Did Not Make Ourselves

We did not make ourselves is one thing
I keep singing into my hands
while falling asleep

For just a second

Before I have to get up and turn on all the lights in the house one after the
   other like opening an Advent calendar

My brain opening
the chemical miracles in my brain
switching on

I can hear

dogs barking
some trees
last stars

You think you'll be missed
it won't last long
I promise

*

I'm not dead but I am
standing very still
in the backyard
staring up at the maple
thirty years ago
a tiny kid waiting on the ground
alone in heaven
in the world
in white sneakers

I'm having a good time humming along to everything I can still remember
    back there

How we're born

Made to look up at everything we didn't make

We didn't
make grass mosquitoes
or breast cancer

We didn't make yellow jackets

or sunlight

either

*

I didn't make my brain
but I'm helping
to finish it

Carefully stacking up everything I made next to everything I ruined in
    broad daylight in bright brainlight

This morning I killed a fly
and didn't lie down
next to the body
as we're supposed to

We're supposed to

Soon I'm going to wake up

dogs
trees
stars

There is only this world and this world

What a relief
created

over and over

Dead Brother Superhero

You don't
have to be afraid
anymore

His super outfit is made from handfuls of oil garbage blood and pinned
    together by stars

Flying
around the room
like a

mosquito

Drinking all the blood
or whatever we
have

to save us
who

need to be saved

*

I whispered   *To the rescue*
and sat
on the dead edge
of my bed
all night and
all morning

My feet did not touch the floor

My heart raced

I counted my breaths like small white sheep and pinned my eyes open
and stared at the door

Any second now

Any second now

*

He saved my brain
from its burning
building

He stopped and started the bullet in my heart
with his teeth

Just like that

He looked down from outer space through all the clouds birds dropping
like weights

He looked out
from the center of the earth
through the fire

he was becoming

in the doorway
and closed his eyes
his cape sweeping
the floor

False Start

At the end of one of the billion light-years of loneliness

My mother sits on the floor of her new kitchen carefully feeding the flies
   from her fingertips

All the lights in the house are on so it must be summer

Wings the color of her nail polish

I like to sit on the floor next to her and tell her what a good job she's
   doing

You're doing such a good job Mom

She's very patient with the ones who refuse to swallow

She hums a little song and shoves the food in

They still have all their wings

It takes a long time because no one is hungry

*

At the end of one of the billion light-years of loneliness

My father trains the flies to walk from one end of his fingers to the other

One fly for every finger

It's going to make him rich

Their brains the color of his brain

All the nerves in your hands getting stepped on at once is very calming

Like being a pine tree

Next he's going to train them to walk across his eyelids

How to hide in the holes in his teeth

When he sings and he never sings we will see wings and brains

*

At the end of one of the billion light-years of loneliness

I stuff my mom and dad into a little red wagon and drag them out into
the ocean

Waves the color of their eyelids

Beach glass

I swim alongside and tell them how good they look

Washed in salt

They haven't seen each other in a very long time so I wait awhile before
hauling them back

Hauling them out of the underworld

The overworld

Dragging them out of their mansions of snow

*

At the end of one of the billion light-years of loneliness

My brother swims out into the ocean with his daughter holding hands
 and talking quietly

Flies drop into the water

His daughter was a fly for a while

Small black and gleaming in the palm of his hand

He blew on her gently and she woke up

Some miracle

He swam out across the waves swinging her screaming above his head
 and looked just like a father

The new daughter

Her new father

*

At the end of one of the billion light-years of loneliness

My brother and I set sail in a red boat

He is almost old and tired so I do most of the rowing

The gods in their mansions are boarding up the windows

Time to move to a different neighborhood

We hold hands in the middle of the ocean and look just like a painting

His paint has just now started to chip away

He needs to be restored

Carefully now

My brother

Flies

Then it's the flies
that wake me
up

It's the flies that gently get me out of bed and slip me into some clothes so
   I can walk around outside

In my body outside
in black and medicine green
in wings

I am tarred and feathered
and walk around
on their legs

all day

It's the flies that sweetly call my name

So I'll know it's time

Walking all over my face
whispering and
eating shit

*

Put on your wings I put on my wings
Slide into your legs
I slide into my legs

Medicine green
Cathedral green
Flying

stained glass windows

My window wings smell like metal and my legs are very thin and can fly
    too you could thread a needle with them

Here we go
through the eye
of a needle

Through all the ten thousand eyes

Your mother's
Your brother's
Your sister's

*

It's my birthday again
for the last time
for a year
again

Thirty-three flies bring in a cake from the other room and set it on fire
    singing the song my name sings

Shoo-wop
shoo-
wop

No one's going to eat this cake

I don't even have any friends anymore

But the flies are my friends

Hold me up in the dark bar
where I drink black beer
pitcher after pitcher

Indian oceans for my birthday

of India ink

*

It's time to drag the family out
so I'll know I'm alive
and do

a little dance

My sister's eyes are green grass
My brother's are green black

My mother's

The flies will have to life-flight me back home when I finish these encores
    and collect my flowers

I lost all my bets
on the living
and the dead-for-now

My brain wants out
it wants to roll around in the backyard
it wants to water the white
roses

*

I love it here
and am never going
to leave

The flies pull back the top sheet and warm up my side of the bed brushing
    my hair out of my eyes with their long thumbs

They smell like light in childhood

Like trees

The flies behind my eyes start to drift off

They sound like static in the leaves

Ten thousand eyes
opening and closing
at once

There there   they begin to sing

The worst part is over

Ralph Eugene Meatyard: Untitled

Is the light supposed to do that?

I put on one scary mask after another and then hung them in the trees
   where they shine like giant floating jellyfish

Milk-filled condoms

Your mother's face

My brother is hanging from the branches

Hanging or swimming

Our T-shirts absolutely blaze

This is why we think God is white

I am shaken in the trees

I am smeared

*

In one wilderness my brother wears a plastic bag over his head and leaps
   from the barn door

In another there's nothing but leaves and needles

Light burns water off the tips of ferns

It looks like a seizure

Sometimes we sit just inside the barn with no heads at all and hold each
   other

That's the best time

No heads at all

My arms around him

His arms

Around me

*

The children are trees

My brother waves from the branches with both hands

A seizure in the solid green air

Relentless resurrection

First I put on the mask that looks like my brother then I put on the other
    mask that looks like my brother

My older monster

The light is puking pure white onto the ground

It can't help it

First it cuts off your hand

Then it cuts off your arm at the elbow

The New Green

To wake up every morning in the pines in your bedroom and have to
    shake off the green nightlights is a blessing

I want to burn down the forest
that's been growing
all night
in my brain

I left a note in my brain in red Sharpie it says   *Don't forget the matches*

Embers go flying up to the top branches

The house
gets brighter and
brighter

Then I call down the hallway to my dead brother

Then more lights

*

In my home in my brain
I'm at home

The pine trees are beautiful and made of green needles the pine trees are
  beautiful and made of green needles

I went to sleep
and when I woke up
I was covered in
pitch

Nothing really happens to you when you're dreaming

Everyone alive is alive
everyone dead is
again

Through the new green
they come back
they can't

come back

but they come back

*

The lights inside the pines
are my pillow

I strike a match on my teeth
and light the needles
I strike the matches
I keep being
alive

I didn't know that it would get easier but it does

The rain softly through the last of the branches is your voice

The lights are my pillow

My brother is my mattress

My mother turns off
the trees
and

tucks us in

Killing Flies

I sit down for dinner
with my brother
again

This is the last dream I ever want to have

Passing the forks
around the table passing
the knives

One thing I want to know is who's in the kitchen right now if it isn't me

It isn't me

The kitchen is full of flies
flies are doing all
the work

They light on the edge of the roasted chicken

The bone china

That's what they do

Light

*

I will look
more and more like him
until I'm older
than he is

Then he'll look more like me
if I was lost

The flies need to be killed as soon as we're done eating this delicious meal
    they made

They serve us anything we want
in toxic tuxedos
and shitwings

My brother and I
wipe our mouths scrape chairs back
from the table and
stand up

These are the last things we'll do together

Eat dinner

Kill flies

*

You have to lie down next to the bodies shining all in a row like black
   sequins stitching up the kitchen floor

It's hard to do
but you have to
do it

Quietly lie down and not sleep

We don't sleep

My brother and I work hard all night

Sticking their eyes
onto our earlobes and wrists
like Egyptian
jewelry

He is my emergency exit

I am his dinner date

Home

In heaven
ants are the doormen
to the flies

I climbed out of one butchered ballroom into another climbing out of my
    half-life into my new life on earth

My brother right behind me

Home

The ants are a straight line
showing us the way
out of here

The flies are a straight line
with wings

They live in shit

We lived in a little blue house with a maple tree in the front yard

One ballroom and then

another

*

I've always wanted my body
to work harder
at being alive

The light you see in veins

Eyelids   eyelids
Snow

Wires in the leaves
eyelids turning red blinking
off and on

My body won't do what I want it to it won't burn

It says   I hold your hands in snow

In my hands

I hold your face

*

What you want to remember
of the earth and
what you end up
remembering

The flies get stuck between the single-pane and the storm windows

Turning the volume up on everything

I could stay here for such a long time

And not go anywhere
not even with you
not even if you were
finally leaving

But your voice
there in front of me
where I am going
to live